100 FACTS
Snakes

100 FACTS
Snakes

Barbara Taylor

Consultant: Camilla de la Bédoyère

Miles Kelly

First published in 2010 by Miles Kelly Publishing Ltd
Harding's Barn, Bardfield End Green, Thaxted, Essex, CM6 3PX, UK

Copyright © Miles Kelly Publishing Ltd 2010

12 14 16 18 20 17 15 13

Publishing Director Belinda Gallagher
Creative Director Jo Cowan
Managing Editor Rosie Neave
Senior Editor Becky Miles
Assistant Editor Claire Philip
Volume Designer Andrea Slane
Image Manager Liberty Newton
Indexer Gill Lee
Production Elizabeth Collins
Reprographics Stephan Davis
Assets Venita Kidwai

All rights reserved. No part of this publication may be reproduced, stored in a retrieval system, or transmitted by any means, electronic, mechanical, photocopying, recording or otherwise, without the prior permission of the copyright holder.

ISBN 978-1-78989-387-8

Printed in China

British Library Cataloguing-in-Publication Data
A catalogue record for this book is available from the British Library

ACKNOWLEDGEMENTS

The publishers would like to thank the following artists who have contributed to this book:
Mike Foster (Maltings Partnership), Ian Jackson, Mike Saunders
All other artwork from the Miles Kelly Artwork Bank

The publishers would like to thank the following sources for the use of their photographs:
t = top, b = bottom, l = left, r = right, c = centre

Cover (front) Imagebroker/FLPA, (wavy lines) A.Rom/ShutterstockPremier, (back) Meg Jerrard/Unsplash
Alamy 6–7(bg) age footstock; 18–19(tc) Jack Goldfarb/Design Pics Inc **Ardea** 15(br) Francois Gohier; 17(cr) John Cancalosi; 26(bl) Chris Harvey **Dreamstime** 17(tr) Picstudio; 23(tr) Sharkegg **FLPA** 10(tr) Norbert Wu/Minden Pictures; 11(tr), 16(l) & 42–43(bg) Michael & Patricia Fogden/Minden Pictures; 38(bg) Colin Marshall; 39(b) Photo Researchers **Fotolia** 8(table bl) Eric Gevaert, (table, tuatara tr) reb, (table br) Vatikaki, (table tr) Becky Stares; 36(bl) Dave Rodriguez **Getty** 9(b) Werner Bollmann/Oxford Scientific; 11(b) David B Fleetham/Visuals Unlimited, Inc.; 24–25 (tc) John Cancalosi/age footstock; 25(b) Carol Farneti Foster/Photodisc; 28(bg) David A. Northcott/Corbis Documentary; 30–31(bg) Digital Vision; 41(t) Morales Morales/age footstock; 47(b) Image Source/Vetta **iStock** 13(t) Ameng Wu; 16(tr) Mark Kostich; 18(bl) Seth Ames; 20(tl) lara seregni; 29(cr) Mark Kostich; 34(br) Eric Isselée; 39(tr) Claude Robidoux; 44(tr) ThePalmer; 46(tr) Roman Lipovskiy **Naturepl** 12(b) Daniel Gomez; 17(bl) Visuals Unlimited; 21(b) Tim MacMillan/John Downer Pr; 47(t) John Cancalosi **Photoshot** 34(tl) Daniel Heuclin; 46(bg) Tony Crocetta **ShutterstockPremier** 2–3(bg) Sanne vd Berg Fotografie

All other photographs are from: Corel, digitalvision, Image State, PhotoDisc

Every effort has been made to acknowledge the source and copyright holder of each picture.
Miles Kelly Publishing apologizes for any unintentional errors or omissions.

Made with paper from a sustainable forest

www.mileskelly.net

www.ircf.org The publishers would like to thank the International Reptile Conservation Foundation for their help in compiling this book.

Contents

Secretive serpents 6
What is a snake? 8
Where in the world? 10
Big and small 12
Snake bodies 14
Scaly skin 16
Colours and patterns 18
On the move 20
Super senses 22
Hunting and eating 24
Teeth and jaws 26

Poisonous snakes 28
Cobras and vipers 30
Crushing coils 32
Boas and pythons 34
Survival skills 36
Courtship 38
Laying eggs 40
Giving birth 42
Myths and legends 44
Save our snakes! 46
Index 48

Secretive serpents

1 Snakes have lived on our planet for more than 120 million years. There are nearly 3000 different species (type) of snake alive today. These spectacular, slithering serpents are superbly adapted to life without legs – the word 'serpent' means 'to creep'. Snakes are shy, secretive animals that avoid people whenever they can and will not usually attack unless they need to defend themselves.

▶ The first snakes to evolve were constricting snakes, such as this huge anaconda, which squeezes its prey to death in its strong coils.

What is a snake?

2 Snakes belong to the animal family group known as reptiles. They are related to lizards, turtles, tortoises, crocodiles and alligators. Snakes may have evolved from swimming or burrowing lizards that lived millions of years ago, and are in fact very distant cousins of the dinosaurs!

3 Snakes have long, thin bodies, with no legs, eyelids or external (outside) ears. They can't blink, so they always seem to be staring. Some lizards also have no legs, but they do have eyelids and outer ears.

▼ More than three-quarters of snake species, such as this python, aren't poisonous.

REPTILE FAMILY

Over half of all reptiles are **lizards** – there are around 6000 species.

Amphisbaenians, or worm lizards, are burrowing reptiles that live underground.

Snakes are the second largest group of reptiles, after lizards. Hundreds of species of snakes are poisonous.

Tuataras are rare, ancient and unusual reptiles from New Zealand.

Crocodiles, alligators, gharials and **caimans** are predators with long, narrow snouts and sharp teeth.

Turtles and **tortoises** have a hard shell on their back, which protects them from predators.

4 Like all reptiles, snakes are covered in waterproof scales. A snake's scales grow in the top layers of its skin to protect its body as it slides over the ground. Scales allow skin to stretch when the snake moves or feeds.

TRUE OR FALSE?

1. Snakes have no eyelids.
2. A snake's tongue is shaped like a spoon.
3. Snakes need to eat five or six meals a day.

Answers:
1. True 2. False, it is shaped like a fork 3. False, snakes don't need to eat often and may eat only five or six meals in a year

▲ Snakes are most closely related to lizards, such as the Komodo dragon. It is the largest lizard in the world and can grow up to 3 metres in length.

5 A snake has a forked tongue that it regularly flicks in and out of its mouth. The tongue is used to taste the air and pick up information about the snake's environment. Only a few animals have forked tongues – such as the Komodo dragon, and some other lizards.

6 All snakes are meat-eaters and swallow their prey whole. Since a snake's body works at a slow rate, it takes a long time to digest its food and so can survive for months without eating. A big snake in the wild may eat only five or six meals in a year.

▼ An African rock python opens its jaws extremely wide to swallow an impala, which is the size of a small deer.

Where in the world?

7 **Snakes live all over the world on almost every continent.** There are no snakes on Antarctica, because it is too cold for them to survive. Snakes rely on their surroundings for warmth so they are most common in hot places, such as deserts and rainforests.

▶ This python lives in the rainforests of northeast Australia. Its waterproof skin helps to stop its body from drying out in the heat.

8 **The greatest variety of snakes live in rainforest habitats.** These warm places contain lots of food for snakes to eat and provide plenty of places to rest and shelter. Rainforests are always warm, enabling snakes to keep their body temperature up, which allows them to stay active all year round.

9 **The most widespread snake in the world is the adder.** This poisonous snake lives across Europe and Asia in a variety of habitats, including cold places. The adder's dark colour helps it to warm up quickly when it basks in sunlight, and it sleeps, or hibernates, through the cold winter months.

◀ Adders usually live in undisturbed countryside, from woodland and heathland to sand dunes and mountains.

▶ The sandy-coloured woma python is well camouflaged in its dry desert habitat (home).

10 **In Australia there are more poisonous snakes than non-poisonous ones.** Australia is home to the taipan snake, which has one of the strongest and most powerful poisons of any land snake. It is very secretive and lives in desert areas where there are very few people, so not many people get bitten.

Taipan

11 **Sea snakes live in warm, tropical waters, such as the Indian and Pacific Oceans.** Most sea snakes can take in oxygen from the water through their skin, but they have to come to the surface regularly to breathe air. When underwater, sea snakes close off their nostrils with special valves.

▶ Sea snakes have glands under their tongues that collect salt from their blood. When the snake flicks out its tongue the salt goes back into the water.

SNAKE HABITAT POSTER

You will need:
pen   paper   pictures of snakes
glue   atlas

Using a pen and paper trace a world map from an atlas. Draw on the biggest mountains, forests and deserts and then draw or stick on pictures of snakes from wildlife magazines or the Internet.

Big and small

12 **The six biggest snakes are all boas and pythons.** They are the boa constrictor, the anaconda, the reticulated python, the Indian python, the African rock python and the scrub python. These snakes all take a long time to warm up and need to eat a lot to keep their massive bodies working.

13 **The longest snake in the world is the reticulated python.** An average adult can grow to around 6 metres in length, but it has been known to grow much longer. This snake has an effective camouflage pattern on its scaly skin to help hide its huge body, so it can lie in wait for its prey without being seen.

14 **The heaviest snake is the anaconda.** This enormous snake can be as thick as an adult human and weigh as much as five children! It lives in the rivers of the Amazon rainforest in South America, where the water helps to support its enormous bulk. An anaconda grows up to an impressive 7 or 8 metres long.

I DON'T BELIEVE IT!
The biggest snake ever to have lived was as long as a bus! Known as *Titanoboa*, it lived in the rainforests of South America around 60 million years ago.

▼ It has taken nine people to support the weight of this 5-metre-long anaconda, from South America.

Reticulated python

15 Some of the smallest living snakes are blind snakes. They burrow underground to feed on insects and other soil-dwelling creatures. Most are about 20 centimetres long. Even the biggest blind snakes only reach lengths of around 60 centimetres.

▶ A reticulated python's head is usually between 20 and 25 centimetres in length.

Adder

Eyelash viper

Western diamondback rattlesnake

Fer-de-lance pit viper

◀ The biggest snakes are over 6 metres long, while the smallest are less than a metre in length.

Black mamba

African rock python

Reticulated python

0 1 2 3 4 5 6 7
LENGTH IN METRES

▶ A Barbados thread snake looks more like a small worm than a snake.

Barbados thread snake

16 The world's smallest living snake is a type of thread snake, and is only 10 centimetres long. It usually lives under rocks on the island of Barbados in the Caribbean and probably feeds on termites. Females lay just one large egg and the young are about half as long as the adults.

Snake bodies

> **SHADOW SNAKES**
> **You will need:**
> old socks   torch   white sheet
>
> Make snake shapes by pulling long socks over your hands and arms. Shine a torch onto the back of a white sheet and move your shadow snakes behind the sheet to tell a scary snake story.

17 Snakes come in different shapes and sizes depending on their environment and lifestyle. They may be short, thick and slightly flattened, like a ground-dwelling rattlesnake, or long, thin and lightweight, like a tree snake. Burrowing snakes have tube-shaped bodies, which help them to slide through the soil.

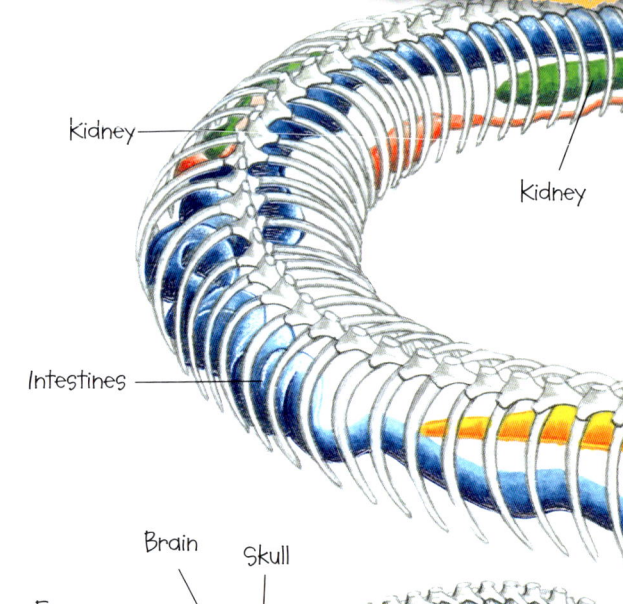

▲ These cross sections show five different snake body shapes, with the backbone and a pair of ribs inside.

18 Some snakes, such as rattlesnakes, have a distinct head and neck region. Others, such as blind snakes, look much the same at both ends. Pythons and vipers have short tails, while the tails of some tree snakes are longer than their bodies.

◀ The Texas blind snake's eyes are two dark spots under three small scales across the top of its head.

▶ A rattlesnake has an arrow-shaped head because of the venom (poison) sacs behind its eyes.

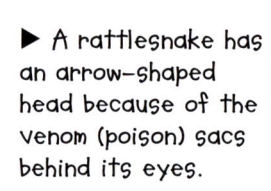

19 There isn't much space inside a snake's body, so the organs are long and thin. Most snakes have only one working right lung, which does the work of two. A snake's skeleton consists mainly of a skull and a long, flexible backbone with up to 400 vertebrae (spine bones).

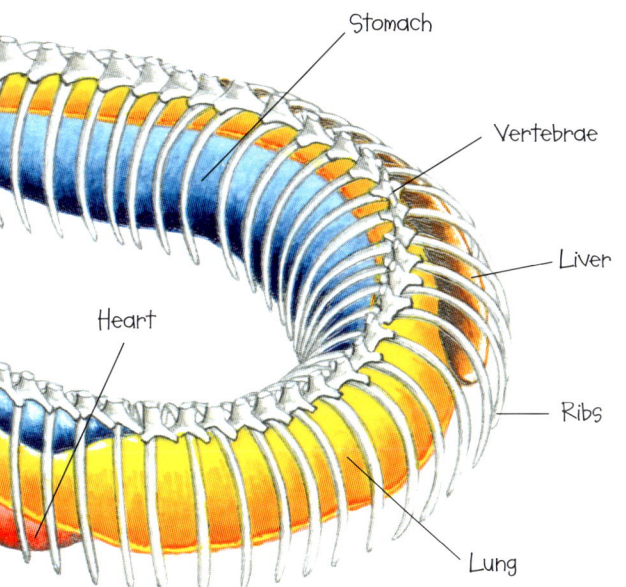

◄ The organs of this male water moccasin are elongated to fit into its long, thin body.

20 Like all reptiles, snakes are cold-blooded. They can't keep their bodies at a constant temperature, the way warm-blooded mammals and birds do. Their bodies stay the same temperature as their surroundings, so they bask in the Sun, or on warm surfaces to gain heat, and move into shade, underground burrows or cool water to cool down.

▼ In cooler parts of North America, thousands of garter snakes often emerge together from their hibernation dens in spring.

21 In colder places, snakes often sleep through the long winter months, waking up in spring when the weather is warmer. This winter sleep is called hibernation. Snakes often hibernate in caves, hollow trees, crevices under rocks or old burrows, where they are protected from the cold winter weather.

Scaly skin

22 A snake's skin is protected by a sheet of dry, horny scales that cover its body like a suit of armour. They are made from thick pieces of keratin – the substance that hair, feathers, nails and claws are made from. Snake scales are linked by hinges of thin keratin and usually fold back, overlapping each other.

▲ Some snakes have 'keeled' scales, with a raised ridge along the middle of each scale.

▲ The areas of skin between a snake's scales allow the body to stretch, making it very flexible.

Head scales

Ventral scales on the underside of the snake's body

Scutes

Dorsal scales on the sides and back

▶ The number, shape, colour and arrangement of a snake's scales helps with identification.

Subcaudal scales under the tail

23 Most snakes have a row of broad scales called scutes underneath their bodies. These scutes go across the snake's belly from one side to the other and end where the tail starts. They help the snake to grip the ground as it moves. Legless lizards don't have scutes, so this is one of the ways to tell them apart from snakes.

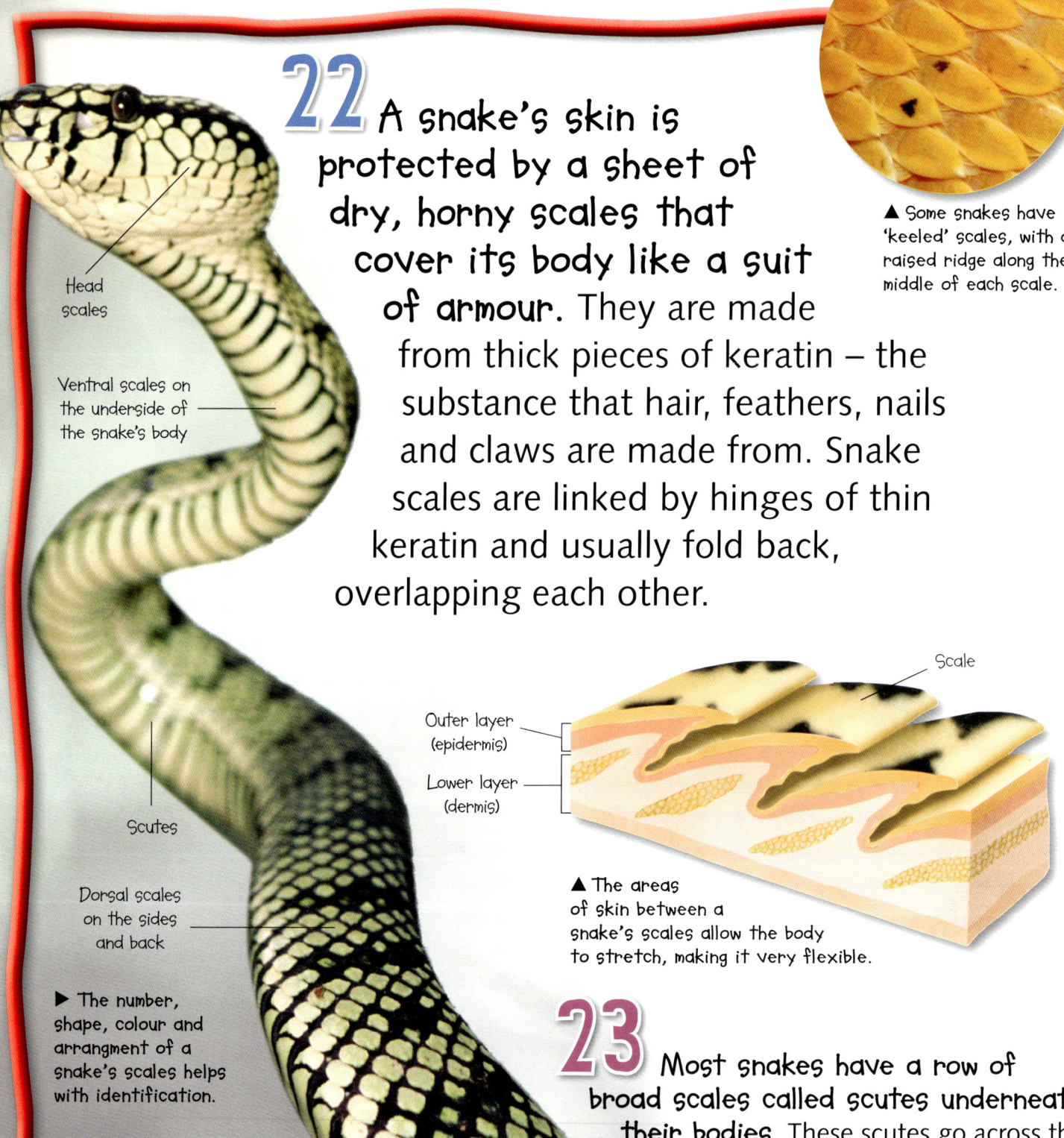

I DON'T BELIEVE IT!

A few snakes polish their scales with a secretion from their nostrils. This may waterproof the scales or allow the snake to leave a scent trail as it slithers along.

24 The texture of a snake's scales helps it to move and catch prey. The scales of coral snakes and burrowing snakes are smooth. This helps them slide easily through small spaces. Wart snakes are covered with rough scales, which help them to grip slippery fish.

25 As snakes move and grow their skin becomes scratched and damaged. Adult snakes slough (moult) their outer layer of skin up to six times a year, but young snakes shed their skin more often as they are growing quickly.

26 A snake's eyes are protected by clear, bubble-like scales. These 'spectacles' or 'brilles' cloud over before a snake sheds its skin. Snakes become sluggish and bad-tempered just before their skin peels off, which may be because they cannot see well and their skin is itchy.

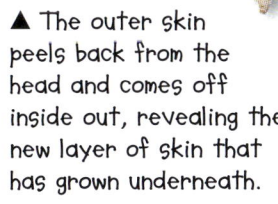

▲ Fluid builds up between the old and new spectacles (scales that cover the eye).

▲ The outer skin peels back from the head and comes off inside out, revealing the new layer of skin that has grown underneath.

◀ The shed skin of a snake is stretched, making it longer than the snake it covered.

Colours and patterns

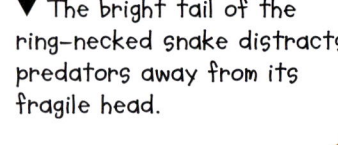

27 **Some snakes are brightly coloured to warn predators that they are poisonous.** There are more than 90 species of coral snake, each with a different pattern of red, black and yellow or white bands. Birds have learnt to avoid snakes with these warning colours.

▼ The bright tail of the ring-necked snake distracts predators away from its fragile head.

28 **Some snakes shimmer with rainbow colours.** Snakes in the sunbeam snake family are named after the way their large, smooth, polished scales create a rainbow effect along their bodies. As they move, light strikes the thin, see-through outer layers of their scales, making their colours appear to change.

◂ The scales of the rainbow boa glimmer with different colours.

SNAKE BRACELET

You will need:
thin card   scissors
colouring pencils   hole punch
wool   beads

Cut a strip of card 20 centimetres long and 3 centimetres wide. Use colouring pencils to draw a snake pattern on it. Punch a hole in each end of the card then tie together with strips of wool. Once you have threaded beads onto the wool and tied a knot in each end it is ready to wear.

29 Some snakes use bright colours to startle or threaten predators. Ring-necked snakes are dull colours on top but have brightly coloured bellies. If threatened, this snake will curl its tail into a corkscrew, creating a sudden flash of colour and drawing attention away from its vulnerable head.

◀ The extraordinary nose shield of the leaf-nosed snake may help to camouflage it while it hunts.

30 Many snakes have colours and patterns that make them blend into their surroundings. Their camouflage helps them avoid predators and catch their prey. Patterns on their scales help to break up the outline of their bodies. The patterns on a Gaboon viper make it look just like the dead leaves on the floor of an African rainforest.

▼ The Gaboon viper is well camouflaged among the leaves as it lies in wait for its prey.

On the move

31 The way a snake moves depends on what species it is, its speed and the surface it is moving over. A snake may wriggle along in an S-shape (serpentine movement), pull half of its body along at a time (concertina movement) or pull its body forwards in a straight line (caterpillar movement).

◀ Tree snakes use an adapted form of concertina movement to move from branch to branch.

32 On smooth or sandy surfaces, snakes move by sidewinding. By anchoring its head and tail firmly on a surface, it can fling the middle part of its body sideways. A sidewinding snake moves diagonally, with only a small part of its body touching the ground at any time.

▼ Sidewinding snakes, such as this viper, leave tracks at a 45° angle to the direction of travel.

33 Tree snakes have strong, prehensile (gripping) tails, which coil around branches. Holding on tightly with its tail, a tree snake stretches forwards to the next branch, and then pulls up its tail. This is a sort of concertina movement.

▲ Large, heavy snakes use their belly scutes to grip the ground and pull themselves forwards.

▲ Most snakes move in an S-shaped path, pushing forwards where their curves touch the ground.

▶ When using concertina movement, a snake bunches up its body (1) then stretches the front half forwards (2), and lastly, pulls up the back half of its body (3).

I DON'T BELIEVE IT!
The fastest land snake is the black mamba, which can move at speeds of up to 16–19 kilometres per hour!

34 Sea snakes swim using S-shaped wriggles, rather like the serpentine movement used by many land snakes. To give them extra swimming power, sea snakes have broad, flat tails, which push against the water and propel them along.

▼ This high-speed photo shows how a paradise tree snake flings its body into the air from a branch to glide for distances of up to 100 metres.

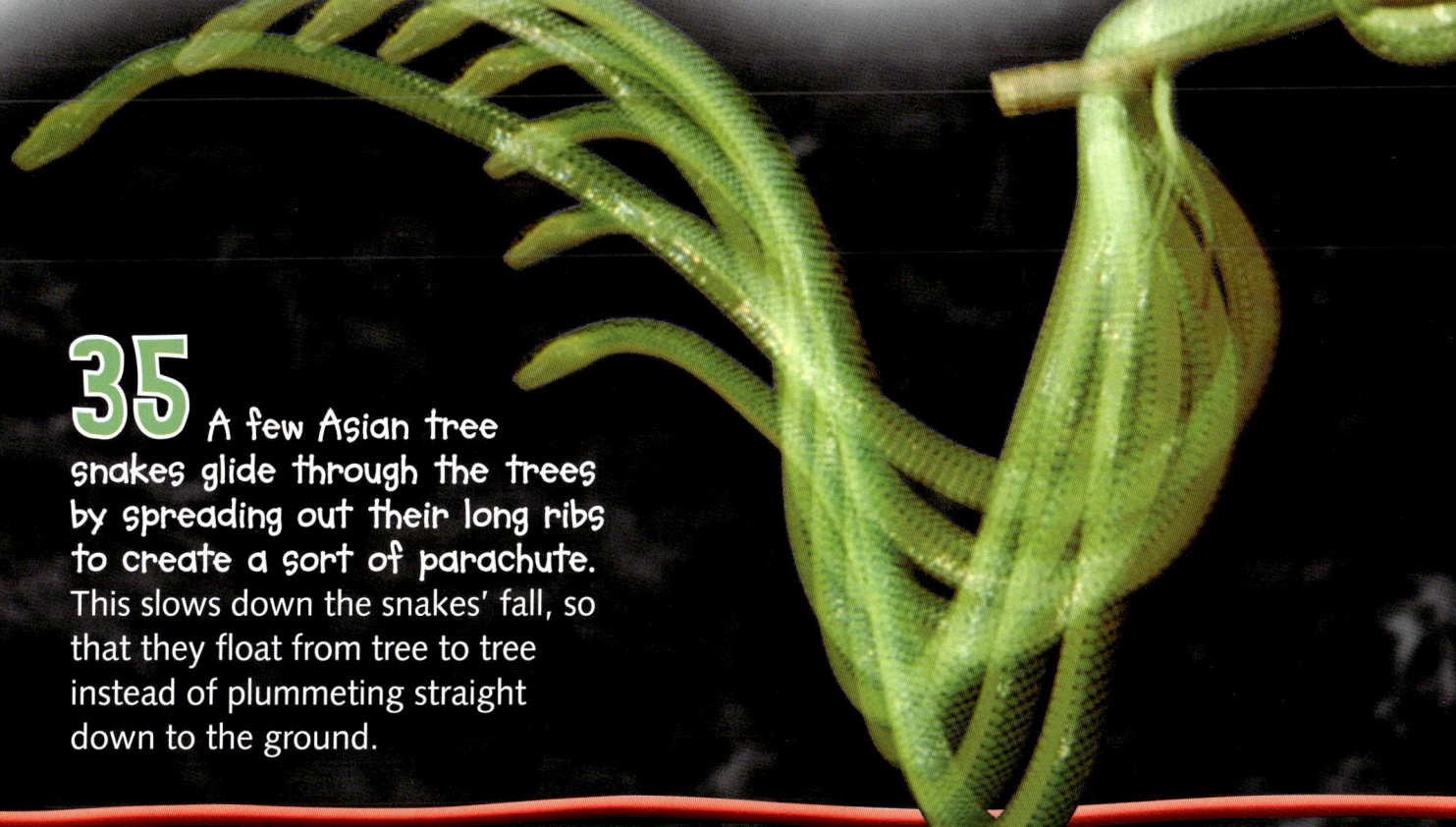

35 A few Asian tree snakes glide through the trees by spreading out their long ribs to create a sort of parachute. This slows down the snakes' fall, so that they float from tree to tree instead of plummeting straight down to the ground.

Super senses

36 Snakes rely on their senses of smell, taste and touch much more than sight or hearing. A snake's tongue is used to collect particles from the air and to touch and feel its surroundings. A snake has a special nerve pit called the Jacobson's organ in the roof of its mouth, which analyses tastes and smells collected by its tongue.

▲ A snake can flick its tongue in and out through a tiny opening even when its mouth is closed. An active snake will do this every few seconds, especially when it is hunting or feels threatened.

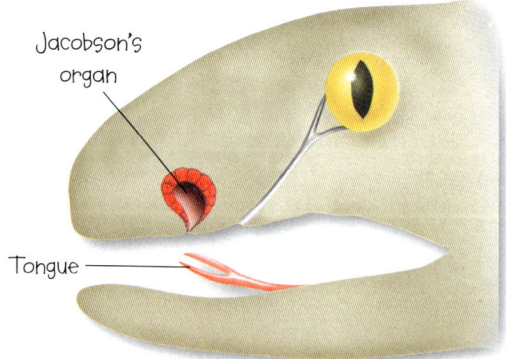

◄ A snake's tongue collects scent particles and chemicals from the air and places them in the two openings of the Jacobson's organ in the roof of its mouth.

QUIZ
1. What is the name of the sense organ in the roof of a snake's mouth?
2. What shape are the pupils of snakes that hunt at night?
3. Why do boas and pythons need to sense heat?

Answers:
1. Jacobson's organ 2. Vertical slits 3. They need to detect the warm bodies of their prey

37 Most snakes have well-developed eyes and some have good eyesight. Some tree snakes have a groove along the snout in front of each of their eyes, so they can see forwards to judge depth and distance. Coachwhip snakes are one of the few snakes to hunt mainly by sight, raising the front end parts of their bodies off the ground.

38 Day-hunting snakes usually have round pupils, whereas night-hunting snakes have vertical, slit-shaped pupils. Vertical pupils can be closed more tightly than round ones, helping protect the snake's eyes from bright light when it comes out to bask in the Sun during the day.

▶ The day-hunting oriental whip snake has a distinctive keyhole-shaped pupil.

▶ The round pupil of a Natal green snake is surrounded by a beautiful golden iris.

▼ By looking along grooves in its narrow, pointed snout, a vine snake can focus both eyes at once, giving it 3D vision.

▶ The eyelash viper has the typical slit-shaped pupil of a night-hunting snake.

39 Snakes have no outer ears or eardrums so they cannot hear sounds in the same way we do. They have an inner ear bone connected to the jaw, which helps them to sense ground vibrations. A snake can also pick up vibrations from the air through its skin.

40 Some snakes, such as pit vipers, boas and pythons, are able to sense the heat given off by their prey. They are the only animals that can do this and their unique sense allows them to track warm-blooded prey, such as rats, in the dark.

Heat pits

◀ Vipers have holes behind their nostrils that are lined with heat-sensitive cells. Boas and pythons have similar heat holes along their lips.

23

Hunting and eating

41 Most snakes eat a wide variety of prey depending on their size, the season and what is available. But a few snakes have very specific diets. Thirst snakes feed only on slugs and snails, queen snakes eat crayfish and children's pythons can move fast enough to catch bats.

▶ The common kingsnake can eat poisonous snakes. It can digest the venom so it is not harmed.

◀ The jaws of an egg-eating snake stretch to swallow an egg three times the diameter of its head.

◀ Once the egg has been swallowed, the snake arches its neck, forcing pointed bones in its throat to break through the shell.

42 An egg-eating snake swallows eggs whole and uses the pointed ends of bones that jut into its throat to crack open the shell. Eggs are a useful source of food because they are rich in body-building protein as well as being easy to find.

◀ The snake then swallows the egg's nutritious contents, and regurgitates (coughs up) the crushed eggshell.

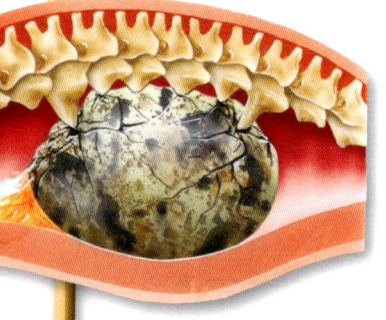

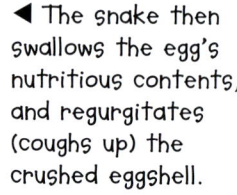

I DON'T BELIEVE IT!

Large snakes can swallow prey up to a quarter of their own length. They have been known to eat leopards, gazelles and even small crocodiles!

44 Many snakes lie in wait to ambush their prey because they cannot move fast enough to chase after it. Snakes such as vipers, boas and pythons have wide bodies so they can eat big meals. They do not have breastbones, so they can move their ribs apart at the front to make their bodies even wider.

45 Some snakes, such as the king cobra, even eat other snakes! A snake's body is easier to swallow than other prey, such as mammals or birds, because it is a thin, smooth shape. Most snakes that eat poisonous snakes are immune to their poisons.

43 Some snakes set traps for their prey. The death adder has a brightly coloured tip to its tail, which looks similar to a worm. The adder wriggles this 'worm' to lure lizards, birds and worms within reach of its poisonous jaws.

▼ Young Mexican cantils have a bright green or yellow tip to their tail. They use this to lure prey, such as frogs, lizards or rodents.

Teeth and jaws

46 Most snakes have short, sharp, curved teeth to grip and hold their prey. The teeth are no good for chewing or tearing up food, which is why snakes swallow their prey whole. A snake's teeth often break as it feeds, but new teeth grow to replace broken ones.

SNAKE BITE!

Snakes want to be left alone. If you see a snake, remain calm, don't panic, keep still and quiet and let the snake go its own way.

When out hiking in areas where snakes live, look where you are going, wear tall boots or hard shoes and don't disturb piles of debris or dark holes.

Never try to pick up a snake — it may bite or spit venom if it feels threatened.

Be aware of how to call for professional help in an emergency and if possible carry an anti-venom kit.

47 Many smaller snakes swallow prey alive, but larger snakes kill their food before they eat it. Around 700 species of snakes use poison, called venom, to immobilize or kill their prey. The venom is injected into the prey through large, pointed teeth, called fangs, which are connected to glands (bags) of venom in the snake's head.

▶ Rear-fanged snakes need to chew their venom into their prey for 15 minutes or more before the poison takes effect.

48 Snakes can have fangs at the front or back of their mouths. Some fanged snakes, such as vipers and cobras, have fangs at the front, while a few snakes, such as the African boomslang, have fangs at the back. Back fangs may either just be large back teeth, or they may have grooves for venom.

Fangs are towards the rear of the mouth, below the eye

▼ Fangs at the back of a snake's mouth help to kill prey as it is being swallowed.

◀ The large fangs of an eyelash viper swing forward to inject venom into its prey.

TRUE OR FALSE?
1. A snake can grow new teeth to replace broken ones.
2. Snake poison is called mevon.
3. Vipers have fangs that can be folded back when they are not being used.

Answers:
1. True 2. False – it is called venom 3. True

49 Snakes in the viper family, such as rattlesnakes and eyelash vipers, have moveable fangs. These can be folded back against the roof of the mouth when they are not in use. When the snake strikes, the fangs swing forwards and bite into the prey, injecting venom deep inside the victim's body.

◀ Most poisonous snakes have hollow fangs at the front of their mouth.

▶ The puff adder has long, folding fangs and strong venom. It is Africa's most dangerous snake.

50 Snakes can open their mouths wider than any other animal, thanks to hinged bones and a stretchy ligament joining the top and bottom jaws. The two sides of a snake's jaw can also move independently of each other, allowing the snake to 'walk' its jaws from side to side as it forces food down its throat, with first one side pulling and then the other.

▶ The red arrow shows how the lower jaw is attached to the skull like a hinge, allowing the jaw to open widely. The blue arrows show how the two sides of the jaw can move backwards and forwards separately.

The lower jaw can stretch wide apart because it is in two halves, joined at the front by a stretchy ligament

Poisonous snakes

51 Venom is a highly modified form of saliva (spit). Saliva is a type of digestive juice, so venom contains enzymes (particles that break down food). These start to digest and soften the meal even before the snake has swallowed it. Snakes don't run out of venom, because their glands make more of this poison as they use it up.

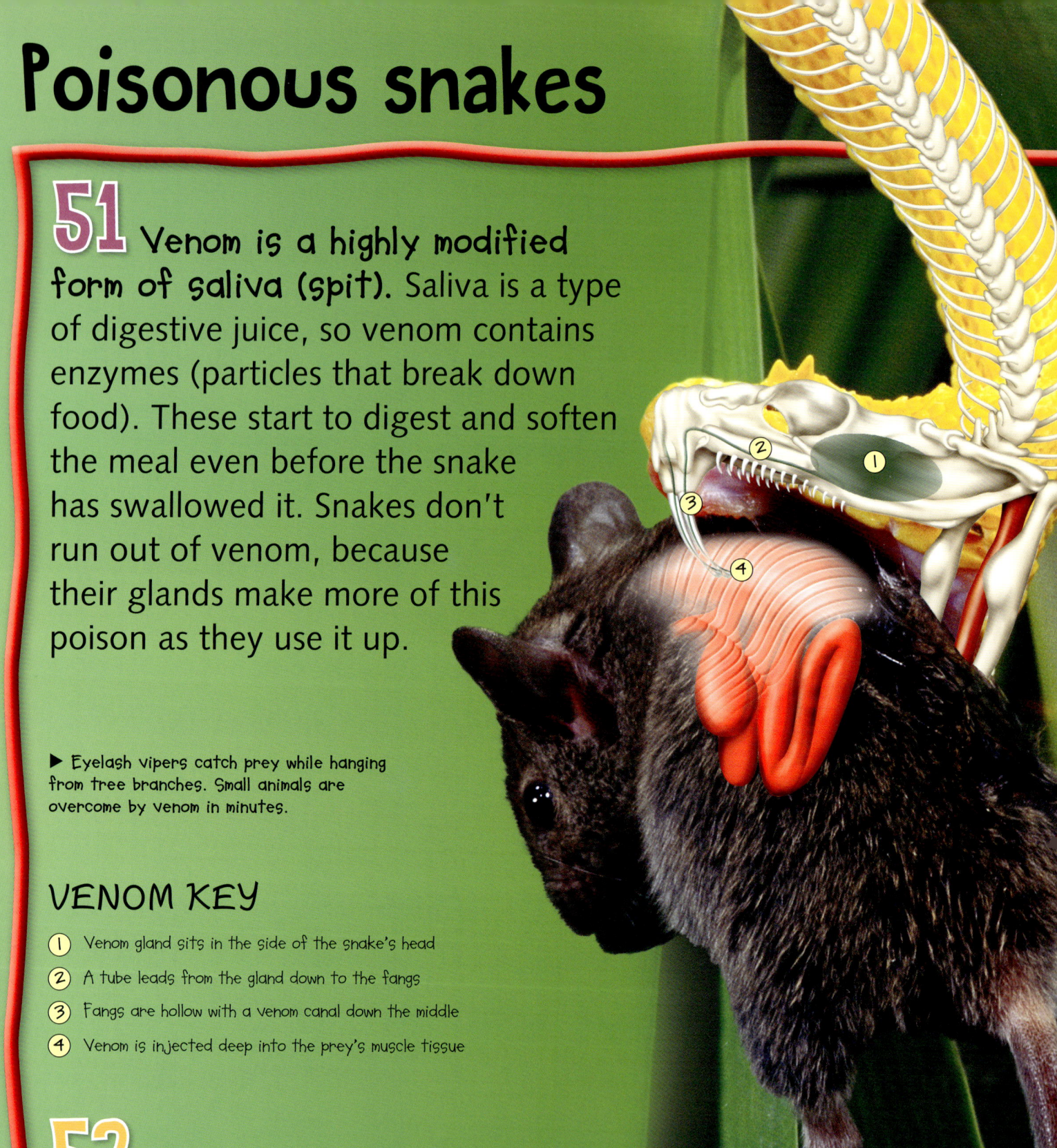

▶ Eyelash vipers catch prey while hanging from tree branches. Small animals are overcome by venom in minutes.

VENOM KEY

1. Venom gland sits in the side of the snake's head
2. A tube leads from the gland down to the fangs
3. Fangs are hollow with a venom canal down the middle
4. Venom is injected deep into the prey's muscle tissue

52 Snake venom is a complicated substance that works in two main ways. Snakes such as cobras, coral snakes and sea snakes have venom that attacks the victim's nervous system, causing paralysis (stopping all movement) and preventing breathing. Snakes such as vipers have venom that destroys body tissues, particularly attacking the circulatory system (blood vessels) and muscles.

53 **Venom is useful because it allows snakes to overcome their prey quickly without being injured.** Snakes with powerful venom, such as vipers, tend to bite their prey quickly and then retreat to a place of safety while their poison takes effect. If the victim crawls away to die, the snake follows its scent trail to keep track of its meal.

▲ The venom of the common krait is very powerful – these snakes are even more poisonous than common cobras.

▼ As the snake bites down, venom flows down its fangs and can be collected in the bottom of a jar.

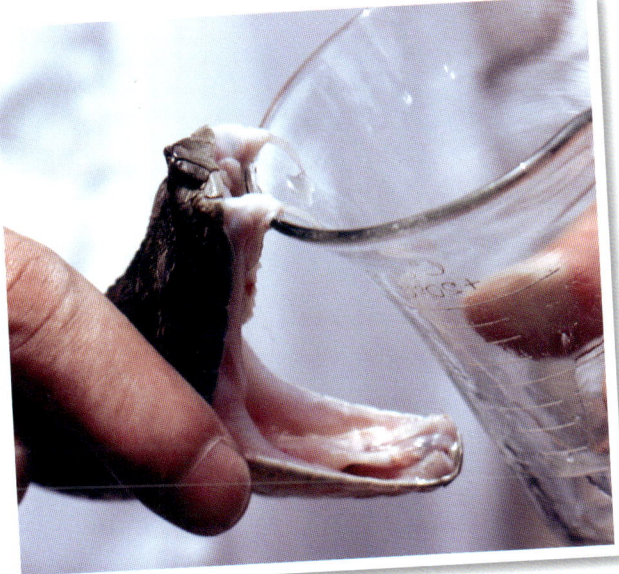

54 **If a person is bitten by a venomous snake the deadliness of the bite varies.** The size and health of the victim, the size of the snake, the number of bites, the amount of venom injected and the speed and quality of medical treatment are important. Some of the most dangerous snakes in the world are the black mamba, Russell's viper and the beaked sea snake.

▶ The black mamba is the longest venomous snake in Africa and is named after the black colour inside its mouth, which it displays if threatened.

55 **Venom is collected from poisonous snakes by making them bite down on the top of a jar.** The venom is used to make a medicine called antivenin, which helps people recover from snake bites. Snake venom can also be used to make other medicines that treat high blood pressure, heart failure and kidney disease.

I DON'T BELIEVE IT!
The king cobra is the world's longest venomous snake, growing to lengths of over 4 metres. Its venom is powerful enough to kill an elephant!

Cobras and vipers

56 The two main groups of poisonous snakes are vipers and elapids. The cobras of Africa and Asia belong to the elapid family, as do the colourful coral snakes of the Americas and the mambas of Africa. Elapids have short, fixed fangs at the front of their mouths, as do their relatives, the sea snakes.

57 Cobras can spread out the skin around their neck into a wide 'hood' that makes them look larger and frightening to their attackers. The hood is supported by long, movable ribs in the cobra's neck. Some cobras have huge eye-spots on the back of the hood, which probably startle predators.

58 To defend themselves, spitting cobras spray venom through small slits in the tips of their fangs. They aim for the eyes of an attacker and can spit venom for distances of up to 1.8 metres – the height of a tall man.

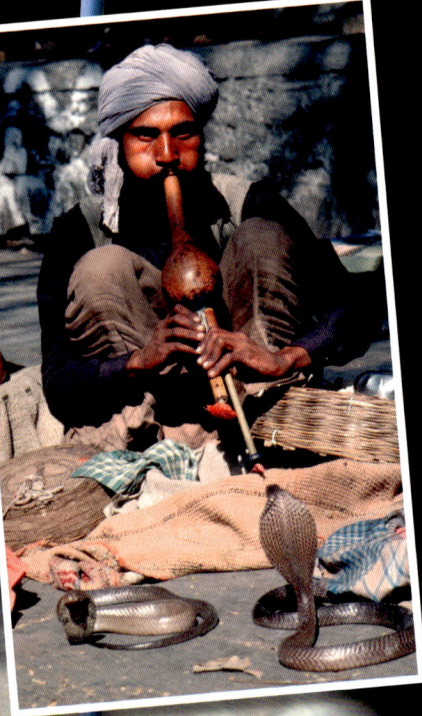

◀ Cobras follow the movement of a snake charmer's pipe. They cannot actually hear the music.

▼ Spitting cobras spray their venom by pushing air out of their lungs while forcing the venom through holes in the front of their fangs.

QUIZ

1. Do cobras have moveable fangs?
2. Why does a puff adder inflate its body like a balloon?
3. How far can spitting cobras spray their venom?

Answers:
1. No, cobras have fixed fangs 2. To defend itself 3. Up to 1.8 metres

59 The viper family of venomous snakes includes the adders, night adders, vipers, bush vipers, rattlesnakes, copperheads, asps and pit vipers. All vipers have long, hollow fangs that can be folded back inside their mouths. The largest viper is the bushmaster, which lives in the forests of Central and South America and grows up to 3.6 metres in length.

▼ The palm viper lives in trees and shrubs, often at the base of palm fronds. Its prehensile tail acts as an anchor.

60 The puff adder inflates its lungs when threatened, which makes its body puff up like a balloon, making it look bigger than it really is. The saw-scaled viper is also named after its threat display because it makes a rasping sound with its jagged-edged scales.

Crushing coils

61 Snakes that squeeze their prey to death by wrapping it tightly in their strong coils are called constrictors. All boas and pythons are constrictors, as are the sunbeam snakes and some of the snakes in the colubrid family, such as rat snakes and kingsnakes.

▼ 1. The snake holds its prey in its teeth and squeezes it to death in its strong coils.

▲ 2. When the animal is dead, the snake opens its mouth very wide and starts to swallow its meal.

62 Constricting snakes usually hold the head end of their prey with their sharp teeth. They then throw their coils around the animal's body and squeeze hard to stop it from breathing. Each time the victim breathes out, the snake squeezes a little harder, until it dies from suffocation or shock.

63 The time it takes for the snake's prey to die depends on the size of the prey and how strong it is. When the prey stops struggling, the snake relaxes its grip, unhinges its jaws and starts to force its meal down its throat.

SPINNING SNAKE

You will need:
paper colouring pencils scissors wool

Draw a spiral on paper and decorate it with stripes or camouflage colours. Add eyes at one end. Carefully cut out the spiral and fix wool to the head end. Hold your snake above a radiator and watch it spin!

64 Prey is usually swallowed head-first. The legs or wings of the animal fold back against the sides of the body and the fur or feathers lie flat – making it easier for the snake to swallow. Slimy saliva in the snake's mouth helps the prey to slide down its throat and into its stomach.

65 When it is swallowing a large meal, a snake finds it difficult to breathe. It may take a long time to swallow a big animal. The snake moves the opening of its windpipe to the front of its mouth so that it can keep breathing while it swallows.

▼ 3. A snake's meal forms a bulge in the middle of its body while it is being digested. It may take days, or even weeks, to be absorbed completely.

Boas and pythons

66 Two powerful types of constricting snakes are boas and pythons. Unlike many other types of snake, most of them have a working left lung, hip bones and the remains of back leg bones. Many boas and pythons have heat-sensitive jaw pits to detect their prey.

67 Many boas and pythons have markings that give them excellent camouflage. The patterns help them to lie in wait for their prey without being seen. The sand boa perfectly matches the rocks and sand of its desert habitat.

▲ The shape of the Kenyan sand boa's mouth and jaws helps it to dig through soft sand.

68 The ball python, or royal python, from West Africa, coils into a tight ball when it is threatened. Its head is well protected in the middle of its coils and it can even be rolled along the ground in this position.

▶ A ball python in a defensive ball shows off its camouflage colours. These snakes can live for up to 50 years.

69 **The emerald tree boa and the green tree python look alike.** These two snakes live in different parts of the world and are not closely related, but they look and behave in a similar way because they both live in rainforest environments.

Emerald tree boa

▲▼ Emerald tree boas and green tree pythons rest in the same way, coiled around branches. They grip tightly with their prehensile tails.

70 **Boas and pythons live in different places around the world.** Most boas live in Central and South America, while pythons live in Africa, southeast Asia and Australia. Another difference between the two snake groups is that all boas (except for one species) give birth to live young, while all pythons lay eggs.

I DON'T BELIEVE IT!
The smallest type of python in the world is the anthill python, which grows to a maximum length of 30 centimetres.

Green tree python

Survival skills

71 Snakes have delicate bodies and are vulnerable to attack from a variety of predators. Animals such as foxes, racoons, crocodiles, baboons and even other snakes will attack them. Predators that specialize in snakes include the secretary bird of the African grasslands, which stamps on snakes to kill them.

72 Rattlesnakes warn predators to keep away by shaking the hollow scales on their tails, making a buzzing sound. Each time a rattlesnake sheds its skin, an extra section of the tail remains, making its rattle one section longer.

◀ A rattlesnake's 'rattle' is a chain of hollow tail tips, which make a warning sound when shaken.

73 Most predators prefer to eat live prey, so the hognose snake and the grass snake pretend to be dead if they are attacked. They roll onto their backs, open their mouths and keep very still until the predator goes away.

▲ Some snakes 'play dead' to trick a predator into leaving them alone.

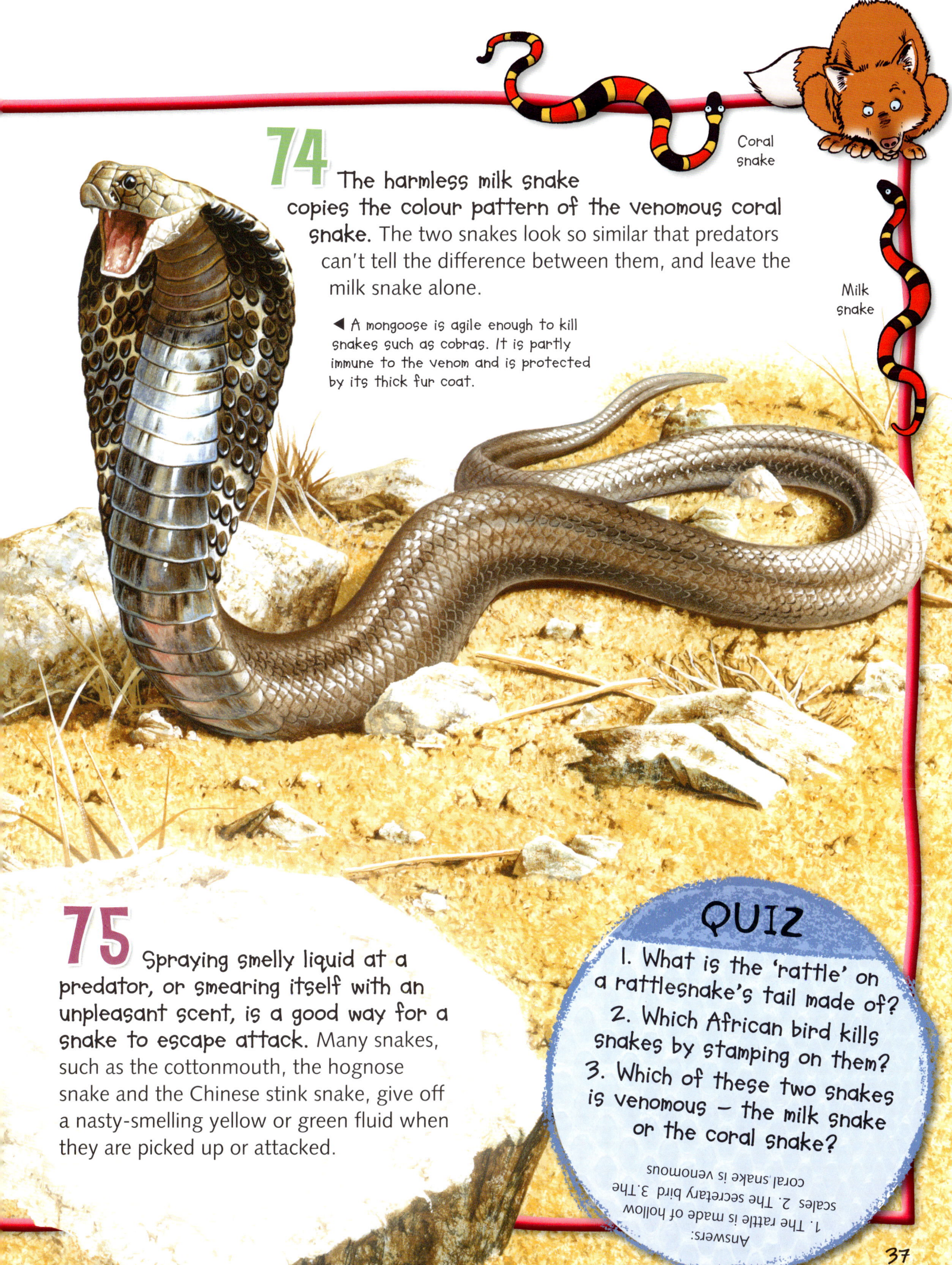

74 The harmless milk snake copies the colour pattern of the venomous coral snake. The two snakes look so similar that predators can't tell the difference between them, and leave the milk snake alone.

◀ A mongoose is agile enough to kill snakes such as cobras. It is partly immune to the venom and is protected by its thick fur coat.

Coral snake

Milk snake

75 Spraying smelly liquid at a predator, or smearing itself with an unpleasant scent, is a good way for a snake to escape attack. Many snakes, such as the cottonmouth, the hognose snake and the Chinese stink snake, give off a nasty-smelling yellow or green fluid when they are picked up or attacked.

QUIZ
1. What is the 'rattle' on a rattlesnake's tail made of?
2. Which African bird kills snakes by stamping on them?
3. Which of these two snakes is venomous – the milk snake or the coral snake?

Answers:
1. The rattle is made of hollow scales 2. The secretary bird 3. The coral snake is venomous

Courtship

76 At certain times of year, usually in the spring or the rainy season, mature male and female snakes search for a mate. They are ready to mate when they are between two and five years old. Male snakes find females by following their scent trails, which signal that they are ready to mate.

▶ Blue-banded sea snakes stay close to each other during courtship and females give birth to between three and five young in the water. The young can swim and feed as soon as they are born.

QUIZ

1. Which snakes use leg spurs during courtship?
2. How long can snake wrestling matches last?
3. At what time of year do garter snakes mate?

Answers:
1. Boas and pythons 2. Several hours 3. In spring, when they emerge from hibernation

77 Male boas and pythons have small spurs on the ends of their tiny back leg bones. They use these spurs to tickle the females during courtship, and also to fight with other males. Females may also have spurs, but these are usually smaller than the spurs of the males.

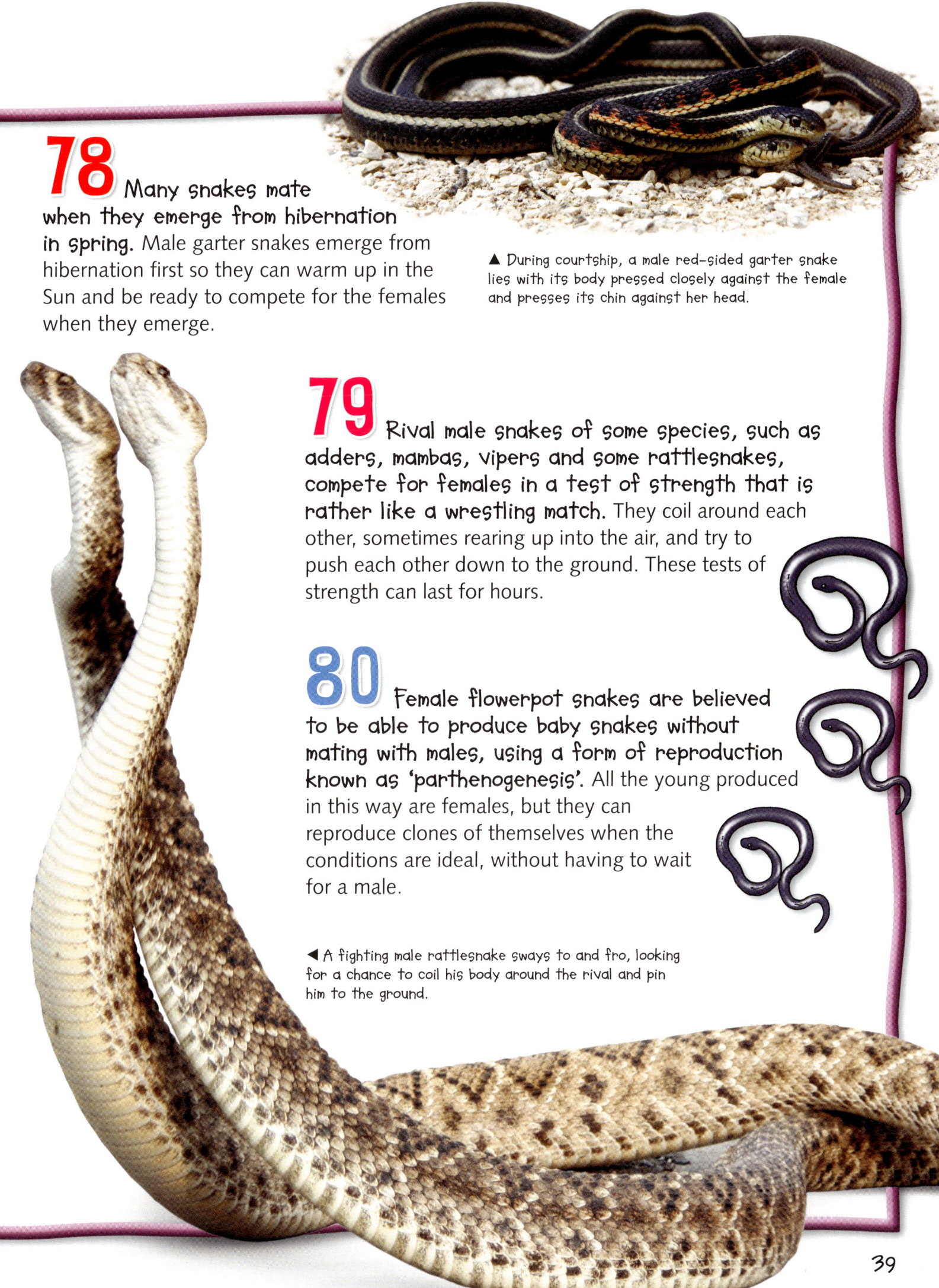

78 Many snakes mate when they emerge from hibernation in spring. Male garter snakes emerge from hibernation first so they can warm up in the Sun and be ready to compete for the females when they emerge.

▲ During courtship, a male red-sided garter snake lies with its body pressed closely against the female and presses its chin against her head.

79 Rival male snakes of some species, such as adders, mambas, vipers and some rattlesnakes, compete for females in a test of strength that is rather like a wrestling match. They coil around each other, sometimes rearing up into the air, and try to push each other down to the ground. These tests of strength can last for hours.

80 Female flowerpot snakes are believed to be able to produce baby snakes without mating with males, using a form of reproduction known as 'parthenogenesis'. All the young produced in this way are females, but they can reproduce clones of themselves when the conditions are ideal, without having to wait for a male.

◄ A fighting male rattlesnake sways to and fro, looking for a chance to coil his body around the rival and pin him to the ground.

Laying eggs

81 About 80 percent of snakes reproduce by laying eggs. A snake's eggshell is tough, leathery, flexible and almost watertight, protecting the developing baby inside from drying out. Female snakes usually lay about five to 20 eggs at a time.

82 Most female snakes don't look after their eggs once they have been laid. Only a few, such as the bushmaster snake, some cobras and most pythons, stay with their eggs to protect them from predators and bad weather.

▼ This cutaway artwork shows a female Burmese python laying eggs. She may lay up to 100 eggs in a single clutch (batch).

TRUE OR FALSE?

1. A snake's eggshell is hard, just like a bird's egg.
2. Pythons are the only snakes that build nests for their eggs.
3. Baby snakes have an egg tooth on their snout to cut slits in their eggshells.

Answers:
1. False – a snake's eggshell is flexible and leathery 2. False – only king cobras are known to build nests for their eggs 3. True

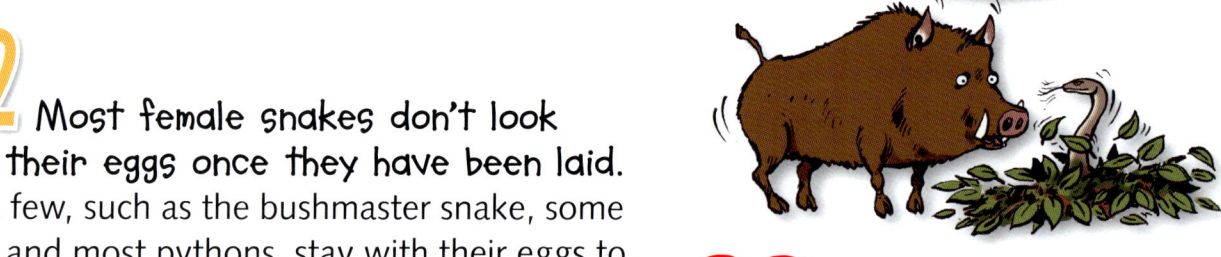

83 The female king cobra is the only snake known to make a nest for her eggs. She builds a mound of rotten leaves, twigs and plant material, lays her eggs in the middle and then perches on top to prevent predators, such as wild boars, from eating them.

84 Female grass snakes and rat snakes lay their eggs in compost heaps or manure heaps. The warmth given off by the rotting plants helps to speed up the development of their eggs.

▲ The grass snake is the only snake in Britain that lays eggs. Females lay 10–40 eggs at a time.

① When fully developed, a baby snake uses the egg tooth on the tip of its snout to tear a hole in the egg.

② The snake tastes the air with its forked tongue. It may stay in the shell for a few days.

③ Eventually, the snake decides to uncoil its slim body and begins to wriggle free of the egg.

85 Baby snakes develop inside eggs for six to 12 weeks, feeding on the yolk stored inside. When it is ready to hatch, a baby snake makes a slit in the eggshell with a sharp egg tooth on its snout. A few hours after hatching, the egg tooth drops off.

④ The baby snake slides along in S-shaped curves to begin its life in the wild.

Giving birth

86 About 20 percent of all snakes give birth to live babies. Boas, rattlesnakes, garter snakes and adders don't lay eggs. Instead, the babies develop inside the mother, and are contained inside clear, tough sacs called membranes instead of shells.

I DON'T BELIEVE IT!
A puff adder in captivity gave birth to 156 babies at one time! This is the largest recorded litter for any snake in the world.

▶ Baby eyelash vipers are about 15–18 centimetres long when they are born. They stay with their mother for about two weeks until they moult their skin for the first time.

The babies have white tips to their tails to lure prey close enough for them to capture

87 Snakes that give birth to live young often live in cold climates. The warmth inside the mother's body helps the baby snakes to develop. The mother can also look for warm places to soak up the Sun's heat, which speeds up the development of her young.

88 Baby snakes that develop inside their mother are better protected than eggs that are laid on the ground. A pregnant snake is heavy, so she often hides away to avoid predators. The extra weight of her developing babies also makes it harder for her to chase prey.

89 Most sea snakes usually give birth to live young, which means they do not have to come onto land to lay eggs. The baby sea snakes are born underwater and have to swim up to the surface to take their first breath. Yellow-bellied sea snakes breed in warm oceans and females give birth to between one and 10 young after five to six months.

90 Most snakes that give birth to live young do not look after their babies when they are born. Venomous snakes are born with their venom glands full of poison, so they can give a dangerous bite to predators soon after birth.

Myths and legends

91 In ancient Greek mythology the hair of the monster Medusa was made of snakes. Anyone who looked at her was instantly turned to stone. The hero Perseus was able to cut off Medusa's head by looking at her reflection in his shield. The drops of blood that fell from the head turned into vipers!

◀ Gilgamesh was probably the ruler of the city of Uruk, from which modern-day Iraq gets its name.

92 In a poem from the Middle East about the hero Gilgamesh, a snake ate a magic plant that could make a person young again. Ever since, so the story goes, snakes have shed their skin and become young again.

▲ Medusa's hair was said to have been turned to snakes as a punishment by the Greek goddess Athena.

93 In the Bible, a serpent in the Garden of Eden persuaded Eve, the first woman, to eat forbidden fruit. Eve gave some of the fruit from the Tree of the Knowledge of Good and Evil to Adam, the first man. God made them leave the Garden of Eden as a punishment.

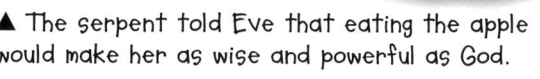
▲ The serpent told Eve that eating the apple would make her as wise and powerful as God.

TRUE OR FALSE?

1. Medusa's hair is made of ropes.
2. Heracles was very good at killing snakes.
3. The story of the rainbow serpent comes from Africa.

Answers:
1. False, Medusa's hair is made of snakes 2. True 3. False, the story of the rainbow serpent comes from Australia

94 Heracles was the son of Zeus, king of the ancient Greek gods. Legend says he strangled two snakes with his bare hands when he was just a baby. The two snakes were sent to kill him by Zeus' jealous wife, Hera, who was not his mother.

95 Traditional beliefs in Australia, India, North America and Africa have linked snakes with rainbows. Rainbows are often associated with rain and new life in different cultures. The Hopi Indians of North America used living snakes in their rain dances and the ancient Chinese also connected snakes with life-giving rain.

▲ The legendary hero Heracles killed a monster called the Hydra. This snake-like creature had nine heads, one of which was immortal.

▲ The rainbow snake is one of the dream-time creatures of the Australian Aborigines. Stories say that he shaped the surface of the Earth with the movements of his body.

Save our snakes!

96 The biggest threat to snakes comes from humans who are destroying their natural habitats. Many snakes are killed by cars and trucks on the road. They are also killed to make tourist souvenirs or for use in traditional medicines.

▲ Some snakes are used to make traditional medicines by soaking them in rice wine, or another type of alcohol.

97 One reason snakes are important is because they control insect and rat populations. To find out the best ways of protecting and conserving snakes, scientists fit them with radio transmitters or tags to mark individuals and collect data about their secretive lives.

▼ Radio-tracking snakes helps conservationists work out why a species is becoming rare and to plan the management of wildlife parks.

98 During the Hindu festival of Nagpanchami, thousands of snakes have traditionally been trapped and killed. Volunteers now rescue the snakes, which are protected by Indian law, and return them to the wild if possible.

SNAKE CONSERVATION

Visit the International Reptile Conservation Foundation's website at www.IRCF.org to learn how conservation groups help save endangered snakes and other reptiles.

99 **The world's rarest snake is probably the Antiguan racer.** The species nearly died out when people introduced rats and mongooses to its habitat. It was also killed by people who wrongly thought it was dangerous. Removing the predators, educating the public and breeding these snakes in captivity may help them survive.

▲ In 1995, only about 60 Antiguan racer snakes survived in the wild. Now conservation efforts have increased numbers to around 300.

100 **There are many rare snakes all over the world.** They include the San Francisco garter snake, which is the most endangered reptile in North America and the eastern indigo, the largest snake in the USA. The king cobra of Asia is rare, as is Dumeril's boa, which is only found on Madagascar. The broad-headed snake is Australia's most endangered snake and the rarest snake in the UK is the smooth snake.

▶ Visting a zoo with snakes is a good way to learn about these fascinating creatures.

Index

Entries in **bold** refer to main subject entries. Entries in *italics* refer to illustrations.

A
adder 10, *10*, *13*, 31, 39, 42
African boomslang 26
African rock python 9, 12, *13*
amphisbaenians 8
anaconda 6, 12, *12*
anthill python 35
Antiguan racer snake 47, *47*
antivenin 29
asps 31

B
ball python 34, *34*
Barbados thread snake 13, *13*
beaked sea snake 29
Bible 44
birth 35, *38*, **42–43**
bites 26, 27, 29, 43
black mamba 13, 21, 29, *29*
blind snake 13, 14, *14*
blue-banded sea snake *38*
broad-headed snake 47
boa constrictor 12
boas 12, 23, 25, 32, **34–35**, 38, 42
bodies 8, 9, 12, **14–15**, *14*, *15*, 16, 18, 20, *21*, 25, 31, *33*, 36, 40, 42
burrowing snakes 13, 14, 15, 17
bush viper 31
bushmaster viper 31, 40

C
camouflage 12, 19, *19*, 34, *34*
children's python 24
Chinese stink snake 37
coachwhip snake 22
cobras 26, 28, 29, **30–31**, *30*, 37, 40
colours 10, *11*, *16*, **18–19**, *18*, 25, *25*, *34*, 37
colubrids 32
common krait 29
conservation **46–47**, 47

constriction 6, **32–33**, 34
copperhead 31
coral snake 17, 18, 28, 30, 37
cottonmouth snake 37
courtship **38–39**, *38*, *39*

D E
death adder 25
deserts 10, 11, *11*, 34
digestion 9, 24, 28, 33, *33*
Dumeril's boa 47
eastern indigo snake 47
egg teeth 41, *41*
egg-eating snake 24, *24*
eggs 13, 24, 35, **40–41**, *40*, *41*
elapids 30
emerald tree boa 35, *35*
eyelash viper *13*, *23*, 27, *27*, *28*, 42
eyes *14*, 17, *17*, 22, 23, *23*

F G
fangs 14, 26, *26*, 27, *27*, 28, 29, 30, 31
fer-de-lance pit viper *13*
flowerpot snake 39
food 8, 13, **24–25**, 26, 28
Gaboon viper 19, *19*
garter snake *15*, 39, *39*, 42
Gilgamesh 44, *44*
grass snake 36, *36*, 41, *41*
green tree python 35, *35*

H
habitats **10–11**, *10*, *11*, 34, 46, 47
Heracles 45, *45*
hibernation 10, 15, *15*, 39
hognose snake 36, 37
hunting 22, *22*, 23, **24–25**

I J K
Indian python 12
Jacobson's organ 22, *22*
jaws 9, *24*, 25, **26–27**, *27*, 33
Kenyan sand boa *34*
keratin 16
king cobra 25, 29, 40, 47
kingsnake *24*, 32
Komodo dragon 9, *9*

L
leaf-nosed snake 19
lizards 8, *8*, 9, *9*

M
mambas 30, 39
medicines 29, *46*
Medusa 44, *44*
Mexican cantil *25*
milk snake 37
mongooses 37, 47
moulting 17, *42*
movement **20–21**
myths **44–45**

N O
Natal green snake *23*
night adder 31
organs 15, *15*
oriental whip snake *23*

P
palm viper 31
paradise tree snake *21*
patterns 12, **18–19**, 34, 37
pit viper 23, 31
poison 8, 10, 11, *14*, 18, *24*, 25, 26, *26*, 27, **28–29**, *29*, 30
predators 18, 19, 30, **36–37**, *36*, 40, 43, 47
prey 6, 9, 12, 17, 19, *19*, 23, 24, 25, *25*, 26, 27, 28, *28*, 29, 32, *32*, 33, 34, 43
puff adder *27*, 31, *42*
pythons 8, *10*, 12, 14, 23, 24, 25, 32, **34–35**, 38, 40, *40*

Q R
queen snake 24
rainbow boa *18*
rainbow snake *45*
rainforests 10, *10*, 12, 19, 35
rat snake 32, 41
rattlesnakes *13*, 14, *14*, 27, 31, 36, *36*, 39, *39*, 42
red-sided garter snake 39
reptiles **8–9**, 15, 47
reticulated python 12, 13
ribs *15*, 21, 25, 30
ring-necked snake *18*, 19
Russell's viper 29

S
San Francisco garter snake 47
sand boa 34, *34*
saw-scaled viper 31
scales 8, 12, *14*, **16–17**, *16*, *17*, 18, *18*, 31, 36
scrub python 12
scutes 16, *20*
sea snakes 11, *11*, 21, 28, 30, 43
senses **22–23**
sidewinding snakes 20, *20*
skeletons 15, *15*
skin 8, 11, 12, **16–17**, *16*, *17*, 23, 30, 42, 44
skulls *14*, 15, 26, 27
smooth snake 47
snake-charming 30
spitting cobra 30, *31*
sunbeam snake 18, 32

T
taipan 11, *11*
Texas blind snake *14*
teeth **26–27**, 32, *32*
thirst snake 24
thread snake 13
tongues 9, 11, 22, *22*, 41
tracking 46, *46*
tree snakes 14, 20, *20*, 21, 22
tuatara 8

V
venom 26, 27, *27*, **28–29**, *28*, *29*, 30, 31, *31*, 37, *37*, 43
vine snakes 23
vipers 14, 19, 20, 23, *23*, 25, 26, 27, 28, 29, **30–31**, 39, 44

W Y Z
wart snake 17
water moccasin *15*
Western diamondback rattlesnake 13
woma python *11*
yellow-bellied sea snake 43
zoos *47*